BOOK ANALYSIS

By Genevieve Zimantas

The Age of Innocence

BY EDITH WHARTON

Bright
≡**Summaries**.com

EDITH WHARTON

AMERICAN NOVELIST, SHORT
STORY WRITER, PLAYWRIGHT,
ACTIVIST, AND DESIGNER

- **Born in New York in 1862.**
- **Died in Saint-Brice-sous-Forêt, France, in 1937.**
- **Notable works:**
    - *The House of Mirth* (1905), novel
    - *Ethan Frome* (1911), novel
    - *The Decoration of Houses* (1897), non-fiction

Edith Wharton was born Edith Newbold Jones to a prominent New York family in the mid-19th century. She travelled throughout Europe frequently in her early life before settling permanently in France after the dissolution of her marriage. Wharton wrote nearly 20 novels and over 50 short stories as well as collections of poetry and plays and was widely recognized during her lifetime for her talent as a writer: she was the first woman to ever win the Pulitzer Prize for literature (for *The Age of Innocence* in 1921) and was thrice nominated for the Nobel Prize.

In addition to her literary career, Wharton was renowned for her expertise in home décor and gardening. She also distinguished herself as an important activist and advocate during the First World War by raising funds for refugees fleeing German occupied Belgium, opening a workroom for unemployed women in France, and editing *The Book of the Homeless* (1915), featuring contributions by Henry James (American-British writer, 1843-1916), Joseph Conrad (Polish-British writer, 1857-1924), and an introduction by Theodore Roosevelt (American statesman, 1858-1919). For these and other efforts France made her a Chevalier of the Legion of Honour and Belgium appointed her a Chevalier of the Order of Leopold.

THE AGE OF INNOCENCE

A PORTRAIT OF AMERICA'S MODERN AGE

- **Genre:** novel
- **Reference edition:** Wharton, E. (1987) *The Age of Innocence*. Harmondsworth: Penguin Books Ltd.
- **1st edition:** 1920 (serialised)
- **Themes:** marriage, gender, wealth, class, love, social criticism, innocence, experience

Often considered Wharton's masterpiece, *The Age of Innocence* traces the growing pains of a modernising American society in 1870s New York against the backdrop of both European society and the history of its fictions. The novel tells the story of Newland Archer's betrothal and marriage to May Welland (later Archer) alongside his unconsummated love affair with her disgraced cousin, Countess Ellen Olenska.

First serialized in *Pictorial Review* in 1920 to great acclaim, *The Age of Innocence* was then published in a single volume by D. Appleton and Company before winning the Pulitzer Prize for literature in 1921, making Edith Wharton the first ever female recipient of the Prize. Never out of print since its first release, Wharton's most beloved novel continues to be widely read and studied. In 1993 it was turned into an award-winning film by Martin Scorsese starring Daniel Day-Lewis as Newland Archer, Winona Ryder as May Welland, and Michelle Pfeiffer as Countess Olenska.

SUMMARY

BOOK 1, CHAPTERS 1-12: NEWS AND A NEW ARRIVAL

The Age of Innocence opens on a night at the opera where, having arrived late, Newland Archer stands at the back of his box and imagines his upcoming engagement and marriage to the beautiful young May Welland. Archer's daydream is quickly interrupted, however, by the arrival of an unknown female figure who joins his betrothed and her family in the audience, settling herself firmly in the gossiping centre of New York society.

Realizing that the woman must be his betrothed's cousin, Countess Olenska, Archer resolves to hasten the announcement of his and May's engagement in order to lend his support to that of his betrothed's family as they welcome their disgraced relative. At a ball soon afterwards, May makes their announcement and the two begin to pay the calls required to cement their social bliss.

During these visits, talk often turns to Countess Olenska's situation and, surprising himself, Archer finds himself defending her right to leave her husband. Inexplicably and increasingly drawn to the subject of everyone's fascination, Archer begins to confront some of his own hypocrisies. His plans for his own marriage and the future, he comes to realize, do not accord with his fundamental belief that a woman should be as free as a man.

Urged by his future in-laws and their lawyer, his boss, and against his own principles, Archer goes to the countess to urge her not to file for divorce in order to forestall further disgrace. She acquiesces to his persuasion and agrees to remain married to avoid further scandal.

CHAPTERS 13-18: THE COUNTESS REFUSES

Chapter 13 begins with another performance no one in Archer's set either watches or enjoys. During a night at the theatre, Archer seeks out Countess Olenska under his fiancée's instruction that he "be kind" (p. 102) to her cousin while she is away on a yearly trip to St. Augustine with her parents.

During the performance, Olenska thanks Archer for his recent advice but is clearly unhappy. Distressed at his part in her unhappiness, Archer asks to meet with her privately again the next day but soon receives a reply confessing that she "ran away" (p. 108) to a mutual friend's home in the country.

Archer follows her to their friend's home where, meeting outdoors, they walk in the cold before taking refuge in a small house on the property. Then, in a moment filled with tension in which Archer wonders if the countess 'ran away' because of her feelings for him, he turns to the window and imagines the "miracle" (p. 114) of her approach behind him.

Countess Olenska does come up behind Archer and slips her hand into his. Just then, however, Archer spots an acquaintance, Mr Beaufort, walking to meet them. The three walk back to the main house together and, irritated at what he suspects is married Mr Beaufort's pursuit of the countess, Archer takes his leave and returns to the city.

Deciding against another meeting when the countess writes to him a few days later, Archer departs instead for St. Augustine where he urges May to move the date up of their wedding. May refuses, however, insisting that he must be rushing into marriage in order to escape feelings for another woman. May is mistaken about whom she believes Archer to love—she suspects a woman with whom he had had an affair before the start of the novel—but forces her fiancé to confront his own feelings.

Back in New York, Archer confesses his feelings to Countess Olenska and promises to give up his engagement. She rebuffs him, citing the impossibility of any future between them, and Book One ends with the arrival of telegrams from May for both the countess and Archer: she writes that she has reconsidered Archer's accelerated timeline, convinced her parents, and set plans in motion for a wedding that spring.

BOOK 2, CHAPTERS 19-34: EVERYTHING RESOLVES EVENTUALLY

Book Two begins with May and Archer's wedding and then jumps to the last leg of their honeymoon abroad. Skipping over long months in which Archer and the countess do not see each other, the narrative picks up again a year into May and Archer's marriage when the latter travels to Boston on business and visits the countess in Washington, where she has been living.

At first, Archer and the countess are stiff in one another's presence but soon fall into their old familiarity, and the countess finally confesses that she does return Archer's love but continues to believe that they made the best decision in avoiding an affair.

Angered with himself for having been so easily deceived about her true feelings, Archer lashes out and eventually proposes that the countess become his mistress since he fears she can never be his wife. The countess evades him and, though she returns to live in New York shortly thereafter, plans to move in with her grandmother so as to protect them both from the temptation.

Resolving to tell May about his love for her cousin and to end their marriage, Archer faces two great surprises towards the end of Book Two: first, that the countess plans to return to Europe; and second, as May reveals on the night of her cousin's farewell party, that she is expecting their first child – a fact that no doubt contributed to the countess's decision to depart.

Understanding that he, like the countess, must do what is best for his unborn child, Archer forsakes his budding plans to follow the countess to Europe and resigns himself to his life with May.

CHAPTER 34: IN LATER LIFE

25 years later, and two years after May's death from pneumonia, Archer travels to Paris with his oldest son. Having learned of the countess from his mother before her death, Archer's son brings his father to visit his great love. Archer, however, refuses to see her. His son goes inside and, after watching from the sidewalk for a few minutes, Archer returns to his hotel alone.

CHARACTER STUDY

NEWLAND ARCHER

Wharton's protagonist, Newland Archer is a wealthy young lawyer engaged to be married at the beginning of *The Age of Innocence*. Nominally employed as a lawyer, Archer is hypocritical about his life and beliefs, aligning himself with the arts and the call for freedom for women while simultaneously admiring his own betrothed most for her 'innocence' and pliability. Drawn to Countess Olenska for her independence and determination, Archer declares his love to her but ultimately follows the life laid out for him by his station. He marries May Welland, has several children, and disappears into the role of his station in social circle.

MAY ARCHER (NÉE WELLAND)

Newland Archer's betrothed and the countess's younger cousin, May Welland is a kind and impressionable young woman. Driven by sympathy for her cousin's plight, she asks Archer to watch out for Countess Olenska and repeatedly puts her betrothed in the way of the other woman. Eventually becoming aware of her husband's true affections, May dutifully raises their children and supports Archer throughout their marriage. She dies of pneumonia after nursing their youngest child back to health 23 years after the main events of the novel, but not before revealing to her oldest son that she knew all along what her husband had sacrificed for her.

COUNTESS ELLEN OLENSKA (NÉE MINGOTT)

May Welland's cousin and the unhappy wife of Count Olenski, Ellen Olenska is the mysterious heart of Wharton's novel and the only character who diverts from the path expected of her in order to honour her own principles. Shouldering the epithet of "poor Ellen Olenska" (p. 14) at the beginning of Book One and with a "pale and serious face" (p. 16) and a "slightly foreign accent" (p. 19), the countess is out of place in the New York society to which she returns and chooses to live amidst the "unmapped quarter inhabited by artists, musicians, and 'people who wrote.'"

(p. 87). Despite her love for Newland Archer, she rebuffs his advances and resigns herself to a life of lonely independence.

MR JULIUS BEAUFORT

A wealthy banker and new arrival to New York's social elite at the beginning of the novel, Mr Beaufort earns Archer's disdain as he tries to pursue Countess Olenska and make her his mistress in the first half of the novel. Rumoured to have been subsidizing her life away from her husband, Mr Beaufort places the countess' reputation and station in further jeopardy in Book Two when, having lost his fortune, he is exiled from the very New York circles to which he had so recently been welcomed.

LAWRENCE LEFFERTS

A well-established member of Archer and May's social circle, Lawrence Lefferts is described as "the foremost authority on 'form' in New York" (p. 11). Unfaithful to his wife, Lefferts is rumoured to have made early advances on Countess Olenska, only to be firmly rejected.

SILLERTON JACKSON

The "authority on 'family'" (p. 12) to compliment Lawrence Lefferts' authority on 'form,' Sillerton Jackson is an elderly character with an encyclopaedic knowledge of all the connections and relationships underpinning the novel's present.

MRS THORLEY RUSHWORTH

Never actually appearing on-page in the novel, Mrs Rushworth is a married woman with whom Archer is known to have been conducting an affair before his engagement to May. Described by the narrator as "'that kind of woman'; foolish, vain, clandestine by nature" (p. 83) and more interested in the idea of an affair than in Archer himself, Mrs Rushworth is credited with having initiated Archer into a male distinction "between the woman one loved and respected and those one enjoyed—and pitied" (*ibid.*).

NED WINSETT

One of the few characters represented in the novel who is not from Archer and May's social class, Ned Winsett is what the narrator describes as a "pure man of letters" (p. 105) forced to turn to journalism to support his family. Living in the same "slum" (p. 104) as the countess, Winsett asks after "the name of the dark lady in that swell box" (*ibid.*) of Archer's in order to thank her for taking care of his son and bringing him home after the boy hurt himself playing near her home. The interaction warms Archer's heart towards the countess even further but also forces him to realize how little he knows about the life, family, or experience of his much poorer friend.

ANALYSIS

INNOCENCE AND EXPERIENCE

Themes of innocence and experience figure heavily in Wharton's Pulitzer Prize-winning novel. Present in the novel's title as well as in its character's conversations, the distinction between those who are innocent and those who are not helps characters to classify and judge one another.

Especially in terms of sexual experience or inexperience ('innocence'), however, these themes expose a deeply ingrained sexism: May is 'good' because she is sexually innocent and will therefore allow Archer the "manly privilege" (p. 10) of initiating her into the worlds of adulthood, marriage, literature, and sex; Countess Olenska, by contrast, is, as a married woman, 'experienced' and therefore an unsuitable match except as a mistress—a role into which several characters seek to relegate her after her arrival in New York.

The firm distinction between innocence and experience as well as the clear privileging of innocence over experience begins to fall apart for Archer, however, early in the novel when he becomes frustrated with what he understands to be the innocence manufactured in his betrothed by "a conspiracy of mothers and aunts and grandmothers and long-dead-ancestresses" (p. 42). Wharton's protagonist gradually admits to himself over the course of the novel that human innocence is a faulty concept, musing that "Untrained human nature was not frank and innocent, it was full of the twists and defences of an instinctive guile" (*ibid.*).

Archer's realization is interesting not only because it represents a clear evolution in his character, but also because it reinforces one of the guiding principles of the novel: that a society which values innocence above all else risks privileging nostalgia over progress and ultimately causes more harm than good.

Indeed, the America represented in Wharton's novel is envisioned by its characters as a "heaven" (p. 68) and a refuge for Countess Olenska, but its puritanical adherence to dated moral codes relegates her instead to the vulnerable position of a woman dependent on men like Lefferts and Beaufort for company—which only risks further besmirching her reputation.

NEW YORK, AMERICA, AND THE 'OLD WORLD'

Repeatedly framing her narrative according to "the custom in New York drawing-rooms" (p. 56) or the habits of "old-fashioned New York" (p. 86), Wharton uses anthropological language throughout *The Age of Innocence* and imbues her narrative with a kind of observational authority.

The novel is decidedly American in its subject and setting and yet, by consistently framing itself and its characters in opposition to the rest of America and to their 'Old World' equivalents like Paris and London, *The Age of Innocence* becomes a markedly international novel, far-reaching in the implications of its ironies.

This false opposition between 'here' (New York) and 'there' (Europe, especially) is evident from the earliest pages of the novel, when the countess is described as strange exactly because of her time spent abroad, but persists throughout the novel and eventually muddies the representation of the very society it professes to depict. Countess Olenska wanted to come "home [...] to be a complete American again" (p. 58) but finds her former home no more welcoming than her adopted one. "I want to do what you all do" she says to Archer in a later conversation, "I want to feel cared for and safe" (p. 65). "But," she acknowledges, "I suppose I've lived too independently" (*ibid.*). New York and its American Dream of freedom and independence exist amongst all the silly displays of pomp and wealth, but only for those whose freedom and independence manifest within socially accepted lines.

For Archer this realization is slow to come but devastating, so that his disillusionment with the city he thought he knew directly parallels his disillusionment with the personal life he had set before himself. "Have you forgotten," Archer asks Countess Olenska early in their acquaintance, "that in our country we don't allow our marriages to be arranged for us?" (p. 57). Archer does not have his marriage arranged for him but, because he conforms to the very social considerations which might have led to such a match in different circumstances, in the end the result is much the same: he marries the best social choice rather than the woman he loves and dooms himself, his wife, and his beloved to the fates of their unhappy lives.

ART AND SOCIETY

Wharton's most famous novel abounds with references to art and its enjoyment: the novel begins at the opera, characters attend the theatre, and talk about purchasing paintings. Archer, especially, references books frequently in his daydreams about the future, imagining how he and his new bride will "read *Faust* together" (p. 10), but also seems to exist within his favourite pieces of literature, "confusing the scene of his projected honeymoon with the masterpieces of literature" (*ibid.*) he so admires.

Archer's appreciation for art at first seems one of his more admirable qualities but it soon becomes clear that he is interested in art in much the same way Mrs Rushworth was interested in him during their affair: more in the idea of the thing than in the thing itself. This admiration for art might therefore be said, instead, to come to represent one of his minor character flaws—betraying an unintended superficiality.

Archer uses books to justify his romantic ideas but, as May knows better than he, they "can't behave like people in novels" (p. 72) (or, rather, in other novels), because they must be responsible for their own reality.

That the reality of Archer's circle is so far removed from that of Olenska and of the "artists, musicians, and 'people who wrote'" (p. 87) who live outside "the small and slippery pyramid which composed Mrs Archer's world" (*ibid.*) is perhaps one of the great tragedies of the novel. Like the artists around her, the countess shows no "desire to be amalgamated within the social structure" (*ibid.*), but Archer, unable to truly perceive the world of art around him, is even less able to understand the quality of different realities around him: he is doomed to misread and to misunderstand even the woman he loves.

FURTHER REFLECTION

SOME QUESTIONS TO THINK ABOUT...

- How does irony function in this novel? In its title?
- What does the narrator mean by framing Newland Archer's early daydreams of marriage as "some scene of old European witchery" (p. 10)? What does this say about the novel's take on marriage?
- What is the role of 'taste' in Wharton's novel?
- What is the significance of the flowers Newland Archer gives to May and Countess Olenska? Are these flowers somehow representative of the women to whom they are given—lilies of the valley and yellow roses, respectively? Or do they reveal more about their sender's perceptions of each woman?
- At the beginning of the novel, everyone in New York society thinks Newland Archer is rescuing Olenska by announcing his engagement when he does and by paying her company. Who

really needs saving at the beginning of the novel? Who really rescues whom?

- How does having a male protagonist impact the way we read this novel? Would the novel have been more effective with a female protagonist? Why or why not?
- Why does Archer compare his wedding to "a first night at the Opera!" (p. 152) with "boxes" (*ibid.*) instead of "pews" (*ibid.*)? How does his imagining of the event as a night at the opera rather than an opera show itself represent an evolution from his early daydreams about marriage?
- How should we read the ending of the novel? Why does Archer refuse to see Countess Olenska? How does the ending impact our reading of the rest of the novel?

We want to hear from you!
Leave a comment on your online library
and share your favourite books on social media!

FURTHER READING

REFERENCE EDITION

- Wharton, E. (1987) *The Age of Innocence*. Harmondsworth: Penguin Books Ltd.

ADDITIONAL SOURCES

- Lee, H. (2007) *Edith Wharton*. London: Chatto and Windus.
- Wharton, E. (1924) *The Writing of Fiction*. New York: Charles Scribner's Sons.

ADAPTATIONS

- *The Age of Innocence*. (1993) [Film]. Martin Scorsese. Dir. USA: Columbia Pictures.

MORE FROM BRIGHTSUMMARIES.COM

- Reading guide – *The House of Mirth* by Edith Wharton.

www.brightsummaries.com

Ebook EAN: 9782808017466

Paperback EAN: 9782808017473

Legal Deposit: D/2019/12603/40

Cover: © Primento

Digital conception by Primento, the digital partner of publishers.